BRIGHT IDEA BOOKS

T0080352

ALIEN
Abductions

by Katie Chanez

CAPSTONE PRESS
a capstone imprint

Bright Idea Books are published by Capstone Press
1710 Roe Crest Drive, North Mankato, Minnesota 56003
www.mycapstone.com

Library of Congress Cataloging-in-Publication Data
Names: Chanez, Katie, author.
Title: Alien abductions / by Katie Chanez.
Description: North Mankato, Minnesota : Capstone Press, [2020] | Series:
   Aliens | Includes index. | Audience: Grade 4 to 6. Identifiers:
   LCCN 2018060987 (print) | LCCN 2019000500 (ebook) | ISBN
   9781543571110 (ebook) | ISBN 9781543571035 (hardcover) | ISBN   9781543574906 (pbk.)
Subjects: LCSH: Alien abduction--Juvenile literature. | Human-alien
   encounters--Juvenile literature.
Classification: LCC BF2050 (ebook) | LCC BF2050 .C463 2020 (print) | DDC 001.942--dc23
LC record available at https://lccn.loc.gov/2018060987

All internet sites appearing in back matter were available and accurate when this book was sent to press.

Editorial Credits
Editor: Claire Vanden Branden
Designer: Becky Daum
Production Specialist: Melissa Martin

Photo Credits
Alamy: AF archive/Paramount Pictures, 15, World History Archive, 9; iStockphoto: AntonioGuillem, 22–23, cosmin4000, 11, 28, goktugg, 31, gremlin, 24–25, Magnilion, 16–17, Mike_Kiev, cover, patrickheagney, 6–7; Shutterstock Images: Fer Gregory, 21, ktsdesign, 5, lassedesignen, 26–27, Linda Bucklin, 18–19, 29, vchal, 12–13

Design Elements: Shutterstock Images, Red Line Editorial

Printed in the United States of America.
PA70

TABLE OF CONTENTS

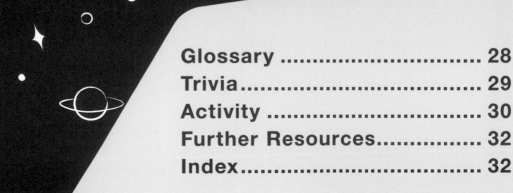

CHAPTER 1

TAKEN

Barney and Betty Hill were driving home in 1961. They had been on vacation. Suddenly a light appeared above them. The light chased their car. They kept driving. But the light kept following. Then they both fell asleep.

Barney and Betty woke up. They were miles away. They could not remember how they got there.

Barney and Betty Hill said they were taken by aliens on September 19, 1961.

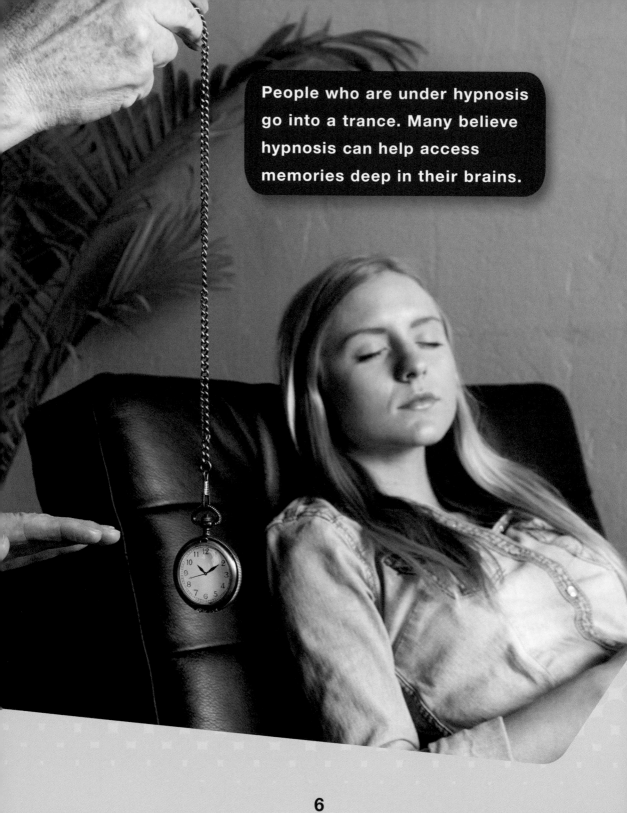

People who are under hypnosis go into a trance. Many believe hypnosis can help access memories deep in their brains.

Betty started having dreams about that night. She dreamed aliens had stopped their car. The aliens brought them onto their spaceship. She could not get this out of her mind.

The Hills decided to see a doctor. The doctor suggested **hypnosis**. It could help them remember what happened to them.

The Hills decided to try it. Afterward they said aliens had **abducted** them. The aliens studied them. Then the aliens took them back to their car. They made Betty and Barney forget what happened.

THE UFO INCIDENT

A movie was made in 1975 about Barney and Betty's abduction. It was called *The UFO Incident*. Reports of alien abductions rose after the movie aired.

The Hills told many people their story.

CHAPTER 2

WHO ARE the Aliens?

Betty said the aliens had gray skin. They had big eyes. They also had small ears and noses. They were about 5 feet (1.5 meters) tall. Barney said they wore black clothes. Many believers call these aliens "Greys."

Believers think
most Greys
have large eyes
and a big head.

GREYS

No one knows for sure if the Greys are real. They also don't know why the Greys take people. Most Greys seem friendly. They let the people go. Betty said one Grey even made a joke.

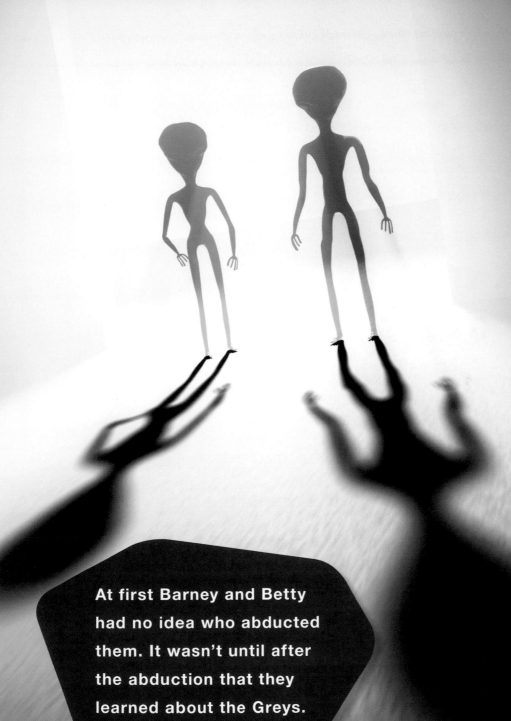

At first Barney and Betty had no idea who abducted them. It wasn't until after the abduction that they learned about the Greys.

NORDICS

The Greys are not the only aliens who are said to take people. Some people say there are aliens called Nordics. They look more like humans than Greys do. They are tall. Sometimes they have blond or red hair. They have been said to take people too.

A movie was made in 1993 about Travis Walton's story. It was called *Fire in the Sky*.

Travis Walton said aliens took him once. They could have been Nordics. He was working in Arizona. One night he and a few men were driving home. They saw a strange light in the sky.

Walton got out to look at it. The men say the light suddenly took Walton.

Walton showed up five days later. He said aliens took him. He woke up on the aliens' spaceship. He later wrote a book about what happened to him.

Walton said that he found the control room on the alien spaceship.

Some people say Reptilians look like lizards.

REPTILIANS

Some people say Reptilians have taken them. These are **shapeshifters**. They have heads like snakes. Most are very tall. They like to hurt people.

CHAPTER 3

ARE PEOPLE Really Taken?

Most scientists don't believe in alien abductions. They say people only think they are taken. This may be because of a sleep condition.

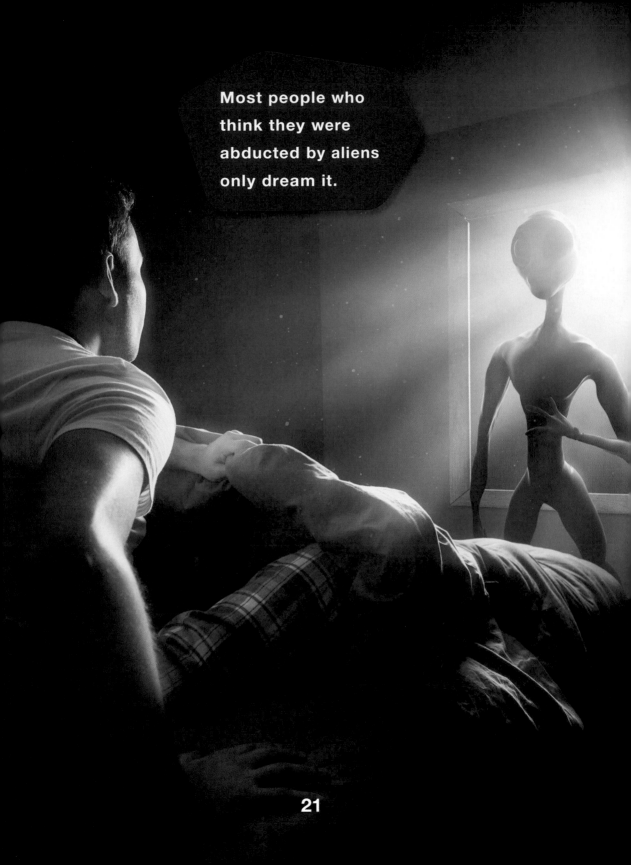

Most people who think they were abducted by aliens only dream it.

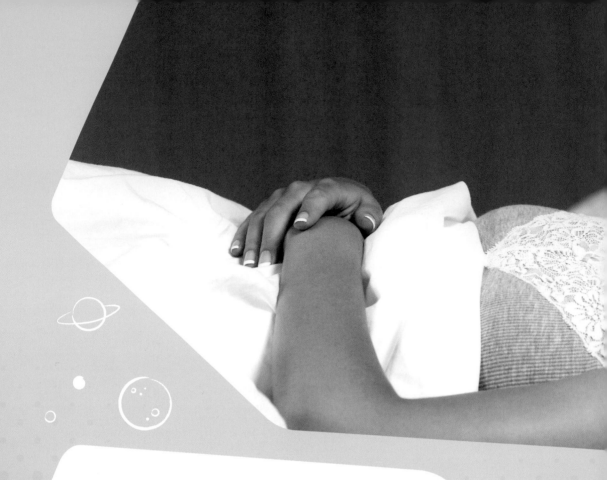

Your body relaxes when you fall asleep. Sometimes people wake up suddenly. They cannot move right away. It can be scary. Sometimes people think they see things that are not there. They are still dreaming.

A person experiencing sleep paralysis cannot move.

Many people who say they were taken do not remember it right away. People can remember things differently. **Hypnotists** can accidentally make people believe things. Sometimes people remember things that never happened.

GREYS ON TELEVISION

Many TV shows and movies show the Greys. One show was on almost two weeks before Barney used hypnosis. Some people think he remembered the TV show.

Hypnosis can sometimes make people think they saw things that never were there.

Most scientists think people have only imagined that they were taken by aliens.

Many people say aliens have taken them. Most scientists think there are other explanations. Believers think scientists are ignoring the truth.

GLOSSARY

abduct
to take a person by force

hypnosis
the process of putting
someone in a trancelike state

hypnotist
a person who puts someone
else under hypnosis

shapeshifter
a person or creature that
can change its physical form
or shape

TRIVIA

1. Betty Hill said the Greys showed her a star map, which she later drew.

2. Some people believe that government officials from around the world are secretly Reptilians, also called lizard people. They think Reptilians want to take over the world.

3. About 6 million Americans have reported being abducted by aliens.

ACTIVITY

CREATE YOUR OWN ALIENS!

Think about the different kinds of aliens mentioned in the book. Now come up with your own aliens. Where are they from? Do they abduct people? Why? What do they hope to do or learn? You can write a story from the point of view of the alien or the human. You could write one side of the story and have a friend write another.

FURTHER RESOURCES

**Want to know more about alien abductions?
Learn more here:**

Martin, Michael. *The Unsolved Mystery of Alien Abductions*. Unexplained
Mysteries. North Mankato, Minn.: Capstone Press, 2014.

**Interested in learning more about aliens?
Check out these resources:**

Chanez, Katie. *UFO Sightings*. Aliens. North Mankato, Minn.: Capstone Press,
2020.

Hile, Lori. *Aliens and UFOs: Myth or Reality?* Investigating Unsolved Mysteries.
North Mankato, Minn.: Capstone Press, 2019.

PBS Learning Media: Search for Extraterrestrial Intelligence: Are We Alone?
https://tpt.pbslearningmedia.org/resource/ess05.sci.ess.eiu.alone/search-for-
extraterrestrial-intelligence-are-we-alone

INDEX